·GUILDF...

'One of the most agreeable and happy looking towns that I ever saw in my life.'
WILLIAM COBBETT

The Land and The Saxons

The high chalk ridge of the North Downs runs from east to west across Surrey. In the west it is cut through by the River Wey, flowing northwards to the Thames. It was in this gap that the town of Guildford grew. In prehistoric times a trackway running along the Downs descended to cross the river in the gap. The resulting ford gave Guildford its name. As settlement developed in what became western Surrey, all the roads and paths converged on the gap to pass through the Downs. A major river crossing at the junction of the local road network would be an obvious place for a town but there is little evidence of prehistoric or Roman settlement.

The first Guildfordians were the people we call the Saxons. Guildford was probably founded about AD 500 by Saxon settlers who named their small community after the 'golden ford' – perhaps referring to yellow flowers nearby or the sand that forms the river bed. These Saxons were pagans, and buried glass beakers and other objects with their dead. They were converted to Christianity in the middle of the 600s and there may well have been a

RIGHT: *St Mary's Church in Quarry Street has a Saxon tower, most of the rest of it being Norman. The chancel was rebuilt in 1825 in order to widen the road where, legend has it, King George IV got stuck in his carriage on the way to Brighton.*

BELOW: *The River Wey Navigation is 25km (15 miles) long with many working locks. It was constructed in the 17th century to bring boats to Guildford from the River Thames. Such was its success that it was extended to Godalming in 1764. The borough received a penny toll on every load coming upstream.*

LEFT: *A Saxon coin of 1066 bearing the image of King Harold. It was struck at the Guildford mint which was set up in the town during the reign of Edward the Martyr (975–978). The coin is on exhibition at the Guildford Museum, Quarry Street.*

wooden church on the site of St Mary's in Quarry Street. In the 900s Guildford developed as a local commercial and administrative centre, with a royal residence and a mint which struck its own coins. In 1036 the town briefly featured in national history with the horrible massacre of the Norman Prince Alfred's followers. Not long after this St Mary's church was rebuilt in stone, and the tower still stands as the only pre-Conquest building to survive in the town.

RIGHT: *Saxon glass cone beakers in Guildford Museum, Quarry Street. These extremely rare beakers were grave goods discovered during excavation of a pagan Saxon cemetery on the Mount.*

Medieval Guildford

It is probable that soon after 1066 William the Conqueror ordered a castle to be built at Guildford. The mound or motte would have been constructed first with a ditch and a timber palisade enclosing a bailey to the south. The motte was probably crowned first by a wooden tower, then by a circular chalk wall. The massive square tower keep was constructed in the mid-1100s both as a residence and as a refuge against attack. Guildford Castle saw little military action though, and became more important as a centre for local government. As the only royal castle in Surrey it became, in the 13th century, the headquarters of the sheriff, who ran the county in the king's name. In particular he was responsible for organizing trials for serious crimes and the keep became the county jail not only for Surrey but Sussex as well. When the royal family came to the castle, they stayed in the palace buildings in the bailey. Of this once-grand royal residence, only the gateway and a few ruins survive.

In 1275 the Dominican Order of Friars set up their friary in the meadows north of the town. It was unusual for such friaries to be built in small provincial towns and testifies to Guildford's importance in medieval times. Like all friaries and monasteries, however, the Guildford friary was closed down by Henry VIII in the Dissolution of the 1530s.

Throughout the Middle Ages Guildford was a small but wealthy town. Its wealth came from the wool trade, introduced into west Surrey by Cistercian monks, who founded Waverley Abbey in 1128. The sheep grazing on the downs and commons around were shorn, the fleeces spun into yarn and then woven into cloth in the villages and farms around. In Guildford the cloth was dyed and finished ready for export. The town was particularly renowned for its 'Guildford Blue' cloth, dyed with woad. Although the wool trade declined and disappeared after the Middle Ages, on the town's coat of arms two woolpacks still flank the castle as a reminder. The 13th-century undercroft below 72 High Street has stonework of the highest quality, and shows the wealth of the merchant who built it.

BELOW: *A late 13th-century undercroft, below a former merchant's house at 72 High Street, has many strange beasts and monsters carved within. These stone-vaulted basements were built as shops when demand for frontages became acute.*

The arms of the Borough of Guildford include the castle and, on each side, a woolpack, indicating the original source of the town's wealth. The town's motto means 'Bravely and faithfully'.

The keep of Surrey's only royal castle was built of sandstone during the reign of Henry II (reigned 1154–89). His grandson, Henry III (reigned 1216–72), made buildings within the bailey into one of the most luxurious royal palaces in the country.

The High Street is the heart of Guildford, descending steeply to the river crossing and up the green slope of the Mount towards Farnham and the west. The street is dominated by the projecting clock of the Guildhall. The hall itself is Elizabethan but probably stands on the site of an earlier building where the Guild Merchant met to run the town's affairs. Henry VII recognized the 'Mayor and Approved Men' as the town's Corporation, which continued until the first elected Town Council of 1835. The frontage of the Guildhall with its bell turret and balconied council chamber was added in 1683. The story is told that a London clock maker, John Aylward, gave the clock in return for the freedom to trade in Guildford.

ABOVE: *A 1778 engraving of the High Street. The most prominent building is the Guildhall on the right, refronted in 1683. Conspicuous by its absence is the portico front of the Cornmarket, later Tunsgate Arch, built opposite the Guildhall in 1818.*

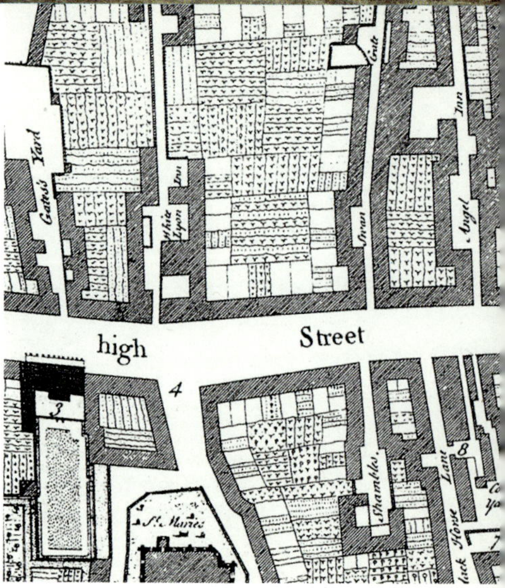

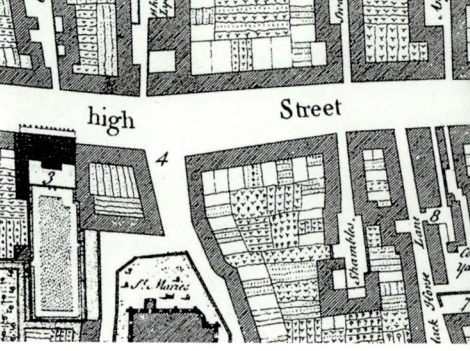

The High Street

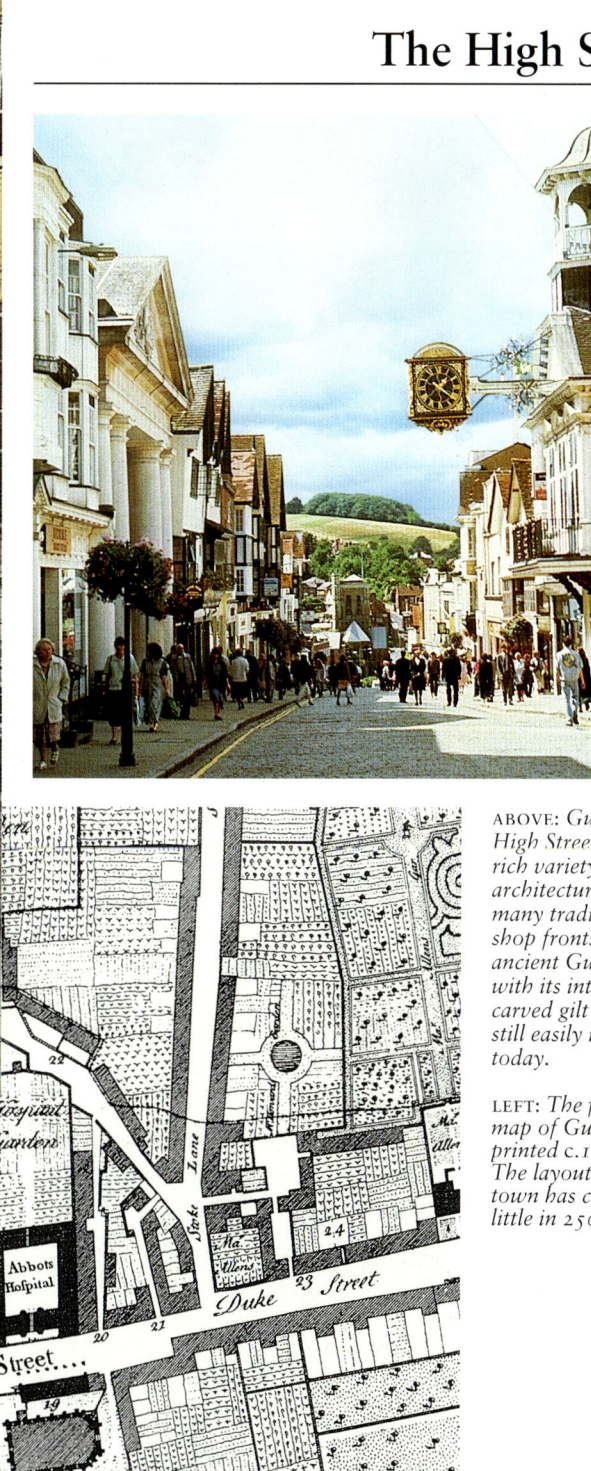

ABOVE: *Guildford's High Street has a rich variety of architecture, with many traditional shop fronts. The ancient Guildhall, with its intricately carved gilt clock, is still easily identified today.*

LEFT: *The first map of Guildford, printed c.1739. The layout of the town has changed little in 250 years.*

The Market Town

BELOW: *The Angel Hotel is the last of the splendid coaching inns for which Guildford was once famous. Much of the traffic from London to the south coast passed through the town, which guards a gap in the Downs.*

Like many provincial market towns there was a grammar school established in Guildford in Tudor times. Founded by Robert Beckingham in 1512, it was re-endowed by Edward VI. 'Grammar' meant Latin and the boys were taught not only to read and write in Latin but also to speak it.

The school produced many distinguished pupils in its early years, but none more so than George Abbot. Born in 1562, Abbot showed himself to be a talented scholar, especially of the ancient languages so vital then to a proper understanding of the Bible. He went to Oxford and helped produce the translation of the Bible we call the Authorized Version. King

James befriended him, making him a bishop and in 1611 Archbishop of Canterbury. With the wealth this position brought him, Abbot decided to build a 'hospital', or almshouse, as a home for elderly Guildfordians. Abbot's Hospital was completed in 1622 in what was then a rather old-fashioned Tudor style. After his death in 1633 a magnificent tomb was built for him in Holy Trinity church, and now a statue has been erected to him. Nevertheless his true memorial is Abbot's Hospital, still in use today for the purpose for which he built it.

BELOW: *A statue of George Abbot (1562–1633), Guildford's most distinguished citizen and benefactor. The son of a cloth worker, he became Vice-Chancellor of Oxford University and later Archbishop of Canterbury. Despite a difficult, later tragic, public life he never forgot the place of his birth, founding the Hospital of the Blessed Trinity, known as Abbot's Hospital, to house the aged poor of the town.*

In Oliver Cromwell's time the river was turned into a canal by cutting off the bends and installing locks. The Wey Navigation made it possible for barges coming up the Thames to Weybridge to travel up the Wey to the town wharf at Guildford. This meant that coal, imported timber and other goods could reach the town cheaply. Also the local farmers could send their produce downstream to the great market of London. The navigation brought a flush of prosperity to the town, but this was badly affected by the collapse of the wool trade in the late 17th century.

ABOVE: *The Royal Grammar School in the High Street was founded in 1512 and re-endowed by Edward VI in 1553. It produced many distinguished scholars including Archbishop George Abbot and his brother Robert, Bishop of Salisbury. Within the school is a rare chained library.*

Travellers and Incomers

Road transport, too, played an increasing part in Guildford's life, particularly when Portsmouth developed as a major naval base from Restoration times. As the town lay halfway on the two-day journey between London and the naval port, many coaches passed through, often stopping at one of the half dozen coaching inns which grew up along the High Street. After the road was 'turnpiked' in 1749, coaches could cover the journey in nine hours. The coming of the railways, however, saw the end of the coaches and one by one the inns closed down. Now only the Angel survives as a reminder of coaching days.

From the mid 1600s to the mid 1800s, Guildford led the quiet life of a small provincial town, acting mainly as the market centre for local farmers. People from as far as mid-Sussex would come to the weekly markets. The varied soil types in the area produced a mixed agriculture, in which sheep and corn were the most important. In 1819, a handsome new corn market was built opposite the Guildhall where wheat, barley and oats were sold.

It was the coming of the railway in 1845 that ushered in a new age. Guildford began to grow as more and more people came to live in the town, now within easy reach of London. One of the new arrivals was Charles Lutwidge Dodgson, better known as Lewis Carroll. He lived in Oxford, where he taught mathematics at Christ Church, but acquired 'The Chestnuts' in Guildford as a home for his brothers and sisters in 1868. It was in this house that he died 30 years later, and he is buried in the Mount Cemetery across the river.

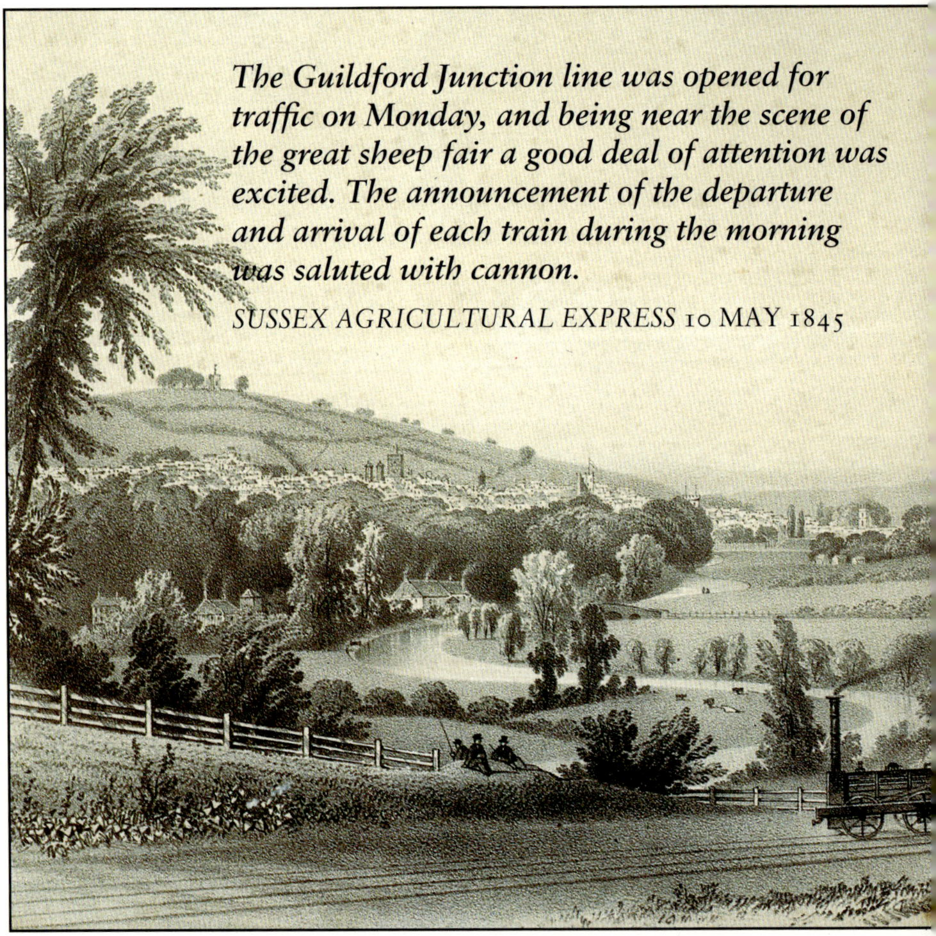

RIGHT: *The railway arrived in Guildford in 1845, a branch of the London & South-Western Railway from Woking. The line's extension only reached Portsmouth in 1859. The Farnham branch, the South-Eastern Railway's Reading to Reigate line, and the London, Brighton & South Coast Railway line to Horsham all served to make Guildford a major junction. Thanks to train travel, townspeople found themselves able to commute to London to work.*

The Guildford Junction line was opened for traffic on Monday, and being near the scene of the great sheep fair a good deal of attention was excited. The announcement of the departure and arrival of each train during the morning was saluted with cannon.

SUSSEX AGRICULTURAL EXPRESS 10 MAY 1845

LEFT: *The statue of Alice Through The Looking Glass (1990) by Jeanne Argent, near the castle. Lewis Carroll taught mathematics at Oxford but was a regular visitor to Guildford, where he rented 'The Chestnuts' on Castle Hill for his six unmarried sisters.*

BELOW: *One of Sir John Tenniel's immortal illustrations from* Alice in Wonderland *by Lewis Carroll. Carroll, who died at Guildford in 1898, refused to acknowledge his connection with anything other than mathematical books!*

ABOVE: *Tunsgate Arch was formerly the entrance to the town's corn market, built in 1818 to resemble a Tuscan temple. It was reconstructed as an arch in the 1930s when Tunsgate was opened to vehicles.*

The Modern Age

LEFT: *Guildford Cathedral, on its splendid hilltop site, was designed by Sir Edward Maufe and built between 1936 and 1961.*

BELOW: *A concert in the cathedral. At nearly 13 metres (41 feet), the nave is wider than in most English cathedrals. The Mendip limestone of the impressive and beautiful interior serves to enhance the shafts of sunlight which grace the cathedral on many days in the year.*

The 20th century saw dramatic growth in Guildford with the construction of large housing estates on the outskirts of the town. The motorcar began to make its presence felt – one of the first by-passes in the country was opened in 1935. Nearby, on Stag Hill, the first cathedral on a new site since the Middle Ages was being built. Guildford had its own bishop from 1927 but the Cathedral of the Holy Spirit was not completed until the 1960s.

After the Second World War, the arts flourished in Guildford, with the Borough Council taking the initiative. The Guildford Philharmonic Orchestra was founded and also the Guildford House Art Gallery, which moved to its present historic building in 1959. A new theatre, named after the local actress Yvonne Arnaud, was opened in 1965.

As well as a cathedral town, Guildford became a university town in 1968 when the University of Surrey was opened on the hill below the cathedral.

The centre of Guildford draws shoppers from a large part of the south east. Recent development has combined successfully with the historic buildings to create a modern town with a great deal of character.